ODD COMFORT

poems by

Michael Darcher

Finishing Line Press
Georgetown, Kentucky

ODD COMFORT

For Joanne who has made so much possible

Copyright © 2022 by Michael Darcher
ISBN 978-1-64662-932-9 First Edition
All rights reserved under International and Pan-American Copyright Conventions. No part of this book may be reproduced in any manner whatsoever without written permission from the publisher, except in the case of brief quotations embodied in critical articles and reviews.

ACKNOWLEDGMENTS

Earlier versions of "The Assassins," "Matriarch," "Catch," "Name Tag," "Another State," "At Christ the King Cemetery," "Roll Call," "When I Was Kicked Out of the Seminary," "Elegy for Bill Hedderly," "Esperanto," "Tri Colores," "The One-Armed Juggler," "Sue Grafton's 27th Novel," "The Periodic Table," and "Damn, I'm Sexy" appeared in various issues of *Crosscurrents*, an annual literary and arts journal published by the Washington Community Colleges Humanities Association.

Publisher: Leah Huete de Maines
Editor: Christen Kincaid
Cover Art: Mike Waller
Author Photo: Mike Waller
Cover Design: Elizabeth Maines McCleavy

Order online: www.finishinglinepress.com
also available on amazon.com

Author inquiries and mail orders:
Finishing Line Press
PO Box 1626
Georgetown, Kentucky 40324
USA

Table of Contents

The Assassins 1

Matriarch 2

When I Was Kicked Out of the Seminary 4

Tri Colores 6

Name Tag 8

Esperanto 9

The One-Armed Juggler 11

Elegy for Bill Hedderly 13

Catch 15

My First and Last Nature Poem 17

Another State 19

Roll Call 20

Sue Grafton's 27th Novel 21

Time Darts 23

At Christ the King Cemetery 25

Damn, I'm Sexy 26

Close Shave 29

The Periodic Table 32

This Dock, My Home 34

THE ASSASSINS

We bought the peas in bulk
at the A & P. The straws we stole
from Smudgy's Luncheonette then ran
to make the matinee where the one
who paid let the other three in
through the alley exit door.

Once the house lights dimmed,
we filled our mouths with chalky peas,
aimed our straws at invisible foes,
and let fly rounds of stinging ammo.
Cloaked in darkness and SurroundSound,
we listened for the yelps of pain,
suppressing our glee, stayed silent
even when the audience laughed
at the comedy we were not watching.

I taste the dust dry peas
whenever I think of Eddie,
now a townie and filtering
his brains through his liver.
Or Vic, who never came back
from Vietnam and is MIA
in Seattle. Or Bruce, who called me once,
wanting to sell me life insurance.

It's the dry dirt of an unwatered plant
I taste whenever you prod unknowingly
some part of me I think is
safely forgotten, and in that moment
I know why I'm uneasy
seated among strangers in darkness.

MATRIARCH

Rose keeps a bottle
of apricot brandy
hidden underneath her bed
like a red-haired lover,
says it's the only cure
but won't say for what.

On the days Nana Rose can't,
or won't, get out of bed,
the apricot stone a warm restraint,
I do her feet. It's a scene
from the New Testament,
Mary Magdalene scrubbing free
the sins of the world
that fly like starlings
into the smoggy tenement
New York sky.

I wash with nubby cloth
and good warm water
the wrinkled pads
that have carried more
than just her weight.
I clip her nails that crumble
like sand from a riverbank
and rub smooth with a stone
each piedmont sole
no longer callused.

Nana Rose waits
until her feet are anointed
with chamomile oil
before she tells me
the things she let go.

I was a good dancer,
she murmurs
and shuffles her feet
as if confessing a sin,
but William wasn't.
So we took up golf.

What Rose likes best
is for me to run my thumbs
down the long crevices
that traverse her soles,
two life lines,
one pliable and stunted,
one manifest and deep.
Only then does she
cease shuffling to
an imaginary song,
her horizontal march
now a dance.

When I am lucky enough
to find the spots
only she knows,
she shuts her eyes,
wraps her ribbon arms
across herself like a present,
whispers into my conch shell ear,
Sell my clothes, Honey,
I'm going to heaven,
and to prove it
spreads her wings.

WHEN I WAS KICKED OUT OF THE SEMINARY
for Kiefel

The rector asked me to explain
my relationship with Jesus Christ,
so I told him, Strictly platonic.
And when I saw his blood
turn to vinegar, I confessed,
We're seeing other people.

Forty days defrocked,
my schoolboy desk as confining
as my new layman's life,
my quid of faith sans quo of hope,
I shed my watch that now kept
someone else's time, gazed
at the crucifix that for thirty years
had hung like Damocles' halo
above my bed. Kneeling
before this cross, I prayed,
You cannot forgive me, Father,
if I have not sinned.

At dinner, Aunt Helen,
deaf as a chalice, thought
I'd said cemetery, asked
while we broke good bread,
Who gets asked to leave a cemetery?
Who did I think I was? Lazarus?
No one, Aunt Helen said,
not even Jesus, ever died twice.

And too few live once
though Helen is right.
No match ever gets relit
because the vernacular of truth
is this: No hope is eternal.
No wick burns longer than
the candle that cradles it.
The self, the mate, the life we want
is not, cannot, will never be.
Mea culpa. Mea culpa. Mea culpa.
It is not the cross we affirm
but the sign of it.

When I was kicked out
of seminary school,
my savior was still
a god of love.

TRI COLORES

The streets below our villa
are not paved. The cars
that navigate them wobble
drunkenly atop the potholes.
We have sent Wayne down
for another twenty kilo bag
of limes and the second cheapest
tequila. The exchange rate
is eleven and a half pesos
per dollar, but we perform
the ten to one American math.
We do not measure our days
by hours but by the number
of margaritas consumed before
dinner, the number of fish tacos
we'll order tonight at Julio's,
the tide.

It is Easter and we are in Sayulita
where even the Beach of the Dead
is crowded, the holiday tents
clinging like dewdrops to
the capricious shade. We body surf
the six foot waves that break
first for the boarders then for us
until one throws Bobby into
the sudden ocean floor just as
I am wading in for my third
swim of the day. The green sea,
the white of Bobby's panic,
the crimson streams of blood
that stripe his face form now
a makeshift Mexican flag.

The shade where we have cast
our beach towels lies below
the villa of a family that speaks
shy English when they beckon
Bobby into their home. Inside,
they dress his broken nose,
bring the anxious rest of us
plates of ceviche and crab salade,
tell us Not necessary, Not necessary
when Joanne brings back as thanks
a cake.

Tomorrow, Mexico will beat the U.S.
two goals to one. Players will forgo
handshakes, the exchanges of jerseys,
their rancor thick as spit. Tomorrow,
we will remain inside our gated villa,
heed the peal of church bells
and shouts of patriotic glee.
Behind these walls that six geckos
cling to, we will make ourselves
another batch of cocktails, listen to
the honking horns, the foreboding joy.
But today, as we guide Bobby, stunned,
ourselves, to our retreat, we know,
as our amigos in their villa know,
how close is the world that spins
around us, and how not necessary
so much of it is.

NAME TAG

Kylee does not
bother
remembering men's
names   she calls
each man
she does not know
Bob   she says half
the men in America are
named Bob   including
the entire state
of Nebraska   no one has
yet
to correct her
Omaha   Kylee says
although
she's never been
there
has a law
requiring men
to carry combs and
part
their hair according to
political persuasion
but
Kylee let it slip
over an Absolut
and lime that she
would move to
Central
Standard
Time in a second
if someone   some
night
would ask her
what name
she calls herself

ESPERANTO

Full of juice and ready for use,
a boy one-fourth my age
tells his friends. When in doubt,
whip it out, advises another
whose face I cannot see.
I have left my keyboard, unable
to shepherd onto the page
my thoughts. On this melting
August night, I have crossed
three Missoula streets, anxious
to trade the snafu of words
for the safety in numbers and
a Dairy Queen sundae.

Behind me in the queue,
two girls, whose fish scale
eye shadow does not age them,
lament a good love gone bad.
He's a pig, says the pretty one,
the kind that seldom speaks first.
They're all pigs, affirms her friend
who looks at me embarrassed
for voicing a truth she thinks
I may have never known.

I want to tell these girls to stow
their anger, that they're right,
of course, we are all pigs,
but that this is not insult
but affirmation, that there lies
in a man's heart hope
to still stir women
in disconcerting ways.

Rather than order a sundae
I won't likely finish, I want to tell
these two why the wild boar
rushes headlong into the thicket
each time he glimpses rustling,
his longing more native than pride.

This is why the boys
who carry like luminaries
their butterscotch dipped cones
pause, the bolder ones, to ogle
girls too old and too wise
to them, girls they know
are beyond their reach,
before returning the attention
of their selfish tongues
to the immediacy of their desserts.
I wait until the boys retreat
to their bicycles that rest on a knoll,
and the girls resume twining
their long, straight hair, wait
until they are beyond earshot before
I explain the difference between us:
The boy scouts, but the girl guides.
It's not the wand; it's the magician.
I never knew my second wife.

THE ONE-ARMED JUGGLER

doesn't suffer fools,
doesn't lack things to do,
doesn't like it when you
request him to juggle
someone else's imbalanced
schemes. The flaming pins,
the mismatched trios of
tennis rackets, bowling balls,
and knives are just gimmicks. He
waits for the sole request
that is never posed, to make
airborne salmon spawn. He

has the softest handshake,
refuses to pat you on the back,
doesn't wait heart in hand,
will not hand it to you or
anyone else. He manages time
better than you, money
better than you,
navigates his Galaxy
across the week's events
while you're still logging on. He

drives a manual shift, won't
take up the handicap spot
or let you pass. He once
hitchhiked to Antarctica. He
wants to do your taxes,
your sister, someone who
will not make him regret
his reliance on cutlery,
or the difficulty of popcorn,

hot, buttered popcorn,
while he waits for the moment
your eyes forget to perform
their inventory, two dogs
in search of a bone
that was long ago buried.

The one-armed juggler
wants what you want
but not for your reason.

ELEGY FOR BILL HEDDERLY
for Debbie and her boys

You posed the question once
Who entertains the entertainers?
after the two of us had comped
the Reno boys to a full day
of distraction, reprieve from ourselves.
In return, we pitched pennies
of appreciation in your direction,
as if your largess were a given, as certain
as the Washoe Zephyr that ran through us
that afternoon. And I told you the sad truth:
No one entertains us. We entertain ourselves.
Or try.

We are at that age when we anticipate
the passing of our parents to occur
in the coming decade, expect it,
as we expect the leaves to drop each fall,
expect the paper to be in the driveway
each morning. There is odd comfort
in this, the preparations we think
we can make, the knowing that, yes,
we all walk the plank someday,
but for now, the toes curled over
the board's edge are not ours.

Which is why the news that Bill,
Sweet Billy, who believed you had to pass
through L.A. to get to heaven, whose
lifeline cleaved a tempest, who
embraced our dreams as if his design,
has come to the end of his board,
has stopped trying, is now the zephyr
that rips through me.

I weigh all this
while pacing the kitchen floor,
attempting to piece together this puzzle
of sub rosa shape and size. I pace
before my optimistic dog who senses
my sorrow but who still wags her tail,
expecting to be walked, to be fed,
to be entertained and believes
I will.

CATCH

My father, whose favorite color was gray,
could shower and shave and be out
of the house in twenty-five minutes.
He rode the Short Line to Manhattan
for twenty-six years, went to work early,
came home late as someone else. This person
planted flasks of Four Roses like land mines
under couch pillows, inside desk drawers.
Sometimes, I could feel the arc of the bottle
and the warmth of the seat when I'd taken
his place. I'd respect his absence
and move to a different seat.
It was like stepping over a grave.

After I grew even with his eyes,
we stopped playing our twilight game
of catch in the backyard,
and he began watching television.
That's what makes horse racing,
he said whenever the Yankees lost.
I can't see it for dust, he said
about all that loomed beyond our hedges.
Only Lawrence Welk could pry him
from the couch, move his shoes,
bring a dry smile to his face.
Now that's music, he said, as if
the rest of us were deaf. He never
drank with other men. He never
danced with my mother.

He faces north in a town he never saw,
on a treeless hillside, a VA inscription
etched into a gray, faceless stone rectangle
that slashes across the freshly mowed sod,
a pitching rubber bolted into the earth,
four corners that frame no epitaph,
just the arc of two dates and
a name that means nothing,
a reminder of our frail legacy.
The flowers we brought the last time
are never there.

Practice makes perfect, he would have said,
but he stopped throwing.
I would have caught anything
with my Rawlings Big-8 glove:
the high bouncers, the hardballs that hurt,
pop flies, fireflies, anything once.
I would have caught them all,
even the rough hop grounders,
kept my chin down, my legs square,
glove sweeping the ground,
eye on the ball, determined,
waiting.

MY FIRST AND LAST NATURE POEM

Give me a break. I'm from New Jersey.
You tell me how a boyhood spent
in the Garden State might prepare me
for the outdoors. Landscape to me
was somebody's shrubbery, not
the brim of the Sawtooth Mountains,
which, upon first view, seemed
in dire need of orthodontic work.
Cormorants, blue heron, turkey vultures
that cast shadows the size of 747s,
I mean, they're all just birds, right?

I didn't get camping. Why would someone
forsake a warm bed and box springs for
a sleeping bag and ground? Where did the joy
come from lugging necessities from car
to campsite along a trodden trail
of dirt and sap and ash? Calling
walking hiking never made the trek
any shorter nor lessened the likelihood
of awakening to a cold and empty dawn.

Okay, there were a few plums
for a twelve-year-old to pluck,
the chance to wield a hatchet,
the allowance from our scoutmaster
to let everything combustible burn
in the gluttonous fires we stoked, but
what began my migration was
an unexpected frozen rain that fell
overnight, which turned us lighter boys
into sleds, granting us freedom from
the wolves and bears whose weight
punctured the crystalline crust, grounding
their flight. It was a morning I fell inside
a snow globe that forever altered
my gravitational pull.

Finally West, I came to learn
starfish are those colors,
that bands of mustangs still traverse
the Silver State, that tumbleweeds really do.
I learned the desert sky doesn't open up
until you flee the city, your creature comforts,
the humbling desert sky that delegates
our small place on this planet.

I still don't like dirt or smoke or bats
or bees, or handling slimy fish, but
I've reached a place where the sky
matters more than skyscrapers. Those
soothsayers who predicted Columbus
would fall off the edge of the world
had no idea how right they were,
and how right Columbus was
to trust not human voices
but the pitch of the beckoning tide.

ANOTHER STATE

A half day's travel brings us
no closer. And when we do stop,
there are no video distractions,
no music with a pulse louder
than our own, just two
attentive bartenders who
watch you apply lip balm,
repin your sagging hair, finger
your glass. They wait to refill
what you won't make empty.

We cross into another state,
one that takes up two pages
in my Rand-McNally, where
an inch of highway
covers little ground.
There is no growth here, no
trees, no shade or dry grass,
nothing to keep your eyes off me.
Still, I see the long shadow
of your desire, hear your heart
that you keep mute beneath
my old college tee shirt
you now claim as yours.
I told you once you liked
to dress like me. That was before
the touches that serve as warnings,
the shouts that drown out reason,
your looks that lend direction.
No reason to love you now
but for the distance.

ROLL CALL

On the first day of class
the professor asked us
to tell her if we wished
to go by another name.
I was dumbstruck. My thoughts
raced around like a balloon
whose knot has come undone.
I had not prepared
for this opportunity
to shed my residue past,
my borrowed Christian name
I could crawl out of
like a snake's skin.

What then? Rex? Champ? Sonny?
Trevor? Lucky? Butch? Slash?
Or maybe something exotic
like Xavier or Jesus or
Maximillian, emphasis on
the million things
I never thought myself
capable of doing.

This is the name I chose:
Imbecile. My allowance that
whenever the professor asks,
What do you think, Imbecile?
I can arch my back, feel
the constraint of my shirt,
puff my chest in swelling pride
and describe in detail
everything I do not know.

SUE GRAFTON'S 27th NOVEL

It wasn't supposed to be this easy,
the struggling writer notion
cool aloe for the combust soul.
But somewhere around the letter D,
the dream became a template,
a shoe store that sells one size,
and the fingers that once danced on keys
now march across stony QWERTY steps,
compelled not by the writer's voice or eye
but the computer's memory that
can save but cannot bring salvation.
The channel these hands now cross
no longer churns current.

So how to heal the healthy?
The first prescription, a placebo,
would have the writer double back, Y,
then X, then W, a field sobriety test
for those who nightly take these turns.
The second cure doubles up: AA
is for American Airlines, Alcoholics
Anonymous, Associates in Arts,
the finite possibilities of license plate
math. BB is for Ball Bearing. Base
on Balls. Bailey Bridge. Bridget Bardot.
The promising writer who once
winnowed the infinite grace of words
from the prosaic now pounds them
like nails onto the page, driven by
her following and her advance.

If writing is an act
of discovery, then the truest writer
would invent a new letter
and its attendant note, perhaps
the gasp of one's first heartbreak,
or the first sound lightning bugs make
at twilight, or the cacophony of smoke.
She'd create new meanings, explain
to the rest of us who long to travel
unpatrolled passages the want
of memory without conscience, or
how one copes upon learning that
nothing softens an artist's soul
more than the recognition.

TIME DARTS

Seems like two people should have
a better song to claim as theirs
than *Whip It*. But any time
those notes escape the radio,
I think of Sue, a worthy winner
in any Kate Moss look-alike
contest, and how we used to pogo
to this song. Skinny, cinched belt Sue,
who once bumped her head on the moon.

That Easter, Jo-mama and I traveled
to Graceland because Jerusalem
seemed too far. Elvis' aunt
was still alive, so the kitchen
was verboten. Instead, we ventured
past the jungle room, visited the grave
whose headstone houses his misspelled
middle name. Afterwards, amused
by the terrible puns applied
to everything the gift shop shelved,
Joanne made up her own:
Return to Sender condoms,
Jailhouse Rock cocaine.

Those were the Reagan years when
for two summers we were the Sultans
of Swing, the Sultans, undefeated
champions of the Reno Swing Shift
Casino Softball League. There must be
twenty-five people on this planet who
anytime they hear this song recollect
a time when we stored silver dollars,
dykes and Ikes, in Crown Royal bags,
had a bowling alley of beers
waiting for us after shift.
The only obligation we had
was to beat the sun to bed.

Rumor has it Jimi's now in Winnemucca
stuffing his paycheck into a machine
or up his nose. Teen-Age Rick,
we know, bled out mid-shift
at Boomtown. The Kroeger brothers,
the Sultans' battery, never found the door
out of Harrah's. Sue? I'm not sure.
After she moved to the lake
and got married and unmarried,
we lost touch. I've stayed married
to Jo-mama who I caught singing
last night in the shower,
Are You Lonesome Tonight?

And for a moment, I was.
How do you tell someone you fell
in love; you didn't go blind?
Or forgetful? It's an old joke,
Nostalgia ain't what it used to be,
but the notes still dance,
and as long as the radio plays them,
I'll still sing my own refrain.

AT CHRIST THE KING CEMETERY

The groundskeeper
has grown seed over
your verdant grave
now mere landscape,
another fitted piece
unlike the fresh graves,
neatly cornered scabs of earth
that lay like trap doors
atop this field of grass and
bunched flowers.

I have forgotten
to bring a bouquet,
No, not forgotten
because the idea never
willed itself true
like all the dreams
you left in disrepair
on your workbench
or on the bus seat beside you,
for twenty-six years
your compromises folded
neatly as sections
of *The New York Times,*
novas of hope imploding
inside your flask.

Below this slant of hillside
where six of us stand
scattered like seeds, we,
the living, scarecrows
unable to dispatch
our calling memories,
a church bell peals,
starlings shrill for their mates,
and a solitary driver
makes her way toward
her next known destination.

DAMN, I'M SEXY

her license plate alerts
strangers. Above this blind boast

Calvin in decal whizzes gleefully,
not a geyser, more a waterfall,

upon the word ADDICTION.
Was this her final drug test,

her anger now advertisement
for the reclaimed veins

that could not just say No?
On the passenger side floor,

two crumpled Taco Bell
bags nose up to each other

like someone else's shoes,
remnants of a midnight meal

she and that guy shared.
The rain her wipers cannot dispel

is the perspiration he licked
off her top lip, laughed

and licked again, rain that seeps
inside windows that won't roll down,

an Oregon reek three cardboard
Christmas trees cannot musk.

On the passenger seat rest
her things now, the cell phone

she uses as seldom as her turn signal,
the backpack full of someone else's plans

for her, the weight of unread books.
Near the entrance to the college,

she waits for a tricked up Honda
that booms out beat, ti-da-boom,

ti-da-boom-boom, to pull out,
waits for this vacated space.

She has never found a spot
this close, had this much time

to do her face, so she measures
her reflection, dabs powder

on the furrows, reddens
lips that bracket words

she will forfeit in class, words
that have no import. She

reaches for the things that rest
where he sat for as long

as it took for her to say Yes.
The depression in the seat

she doesn't see as tired springs
but the weight of every promise

unfulfilled: the guy, the jokes
she didn't get, the sodden night.

In their place sag the ten pounds
she has not shed in a decade.

She unfastens her restraints, still
victim to the gravity of want,

unaware she will never be
more beautiful than now.

CLOSE SHAVE

Just once, could I shave
like the men with the cleft chins do
in the commercials, their twin blades
shredding through confetti snow
like Bode Miller's skis, his piston legs
and rigid hips forming the perfect sign
of Pi, the equation of spirit over fear,
as determined as his will to win,
as resolute as a game of chicken
between two teenage boys.

As teenage boys, snow fell as money,
and on a good day, once the storm ceased,
the sun now a glint on our red, metal shovels,
my brother Ed and I could make barren two,
maybe three driveways, our negotiations based
on the weight of the snow, the length
of the driveway, the prearranged generosity
of the owner. The conversation always began
on how bad a winter it's been.

How bad a winter it's been is all
anyone can proffer who doesn't know
the other person better. They're not the one
driving you to the airport, you bound
for Azerbaijan, a word pleasing to say
but not ponder. You'll be gone all winter
on a Fulbright, teaching in Baku, a city
of now two million and one. You want me
to visit and want to know when. Istanbul,
I propose instead, and when our friends ask
the same thing, I offer to cart them back
a rug. I repeat this jest to anyone who asks,

avoiding like a skier would a tree
the inference that I don't care or you
haven't asked. On our way to Seatac,
we slalom past the possibility of my visit.
We note the pending snow, and I confess
the reason I never learned to ski, as if
I'm telling you the truth, is my fear
of meting Sonny Bono's fate.

The truth is, in any other life but ours,
I'd gladly assume Sonny Bono's lot, all
but the one standing spruce that felled him.
In your absence (Is this what we both fear?)
I'd gladly have privy to all the Chers
of the world, Cher and Chers alike, aliking me,
their slender fingers plump with rings,
traversing my freshly shaven face. I'd gladly
serve proxy to everyone I represent,
blindful in their trust of me.
I got you, Babe, and you got me. Vote
for me and I'll set you free,
my abiding charge eager to trust
every promise I make.

The promise I cannot make at this
or any moment is that I'll ever come
to Istanbul. It's not the fear of breaking
my word. It's the lack of one. I don't know
why I don't want to see Istanbul or Baku
or Azerbaijan any more than I know
the next time it's going to snow. So when
I place your bag at the airport curb,
embrace you for a final time this season,
I explain the best way to shovel snow.

Make a lane down the middle
then plow each unwanted load,
row by row, to the macadam's edge.
I do the same when I shave, start
at my philtrum, work in rows
toward one ear then the other,
scrape in scored lines the downhill
runs of my chin. My life without you
is a badly written song, an infomercial
promising two of the same items
no one wants, a reflection no one sees.

Just once, what I'd like to see reflected,
razor clenched like a tomahawk, poised
to strike at the enemy within, are
two eyes in cocksure agreement
lodged in the sanctuary of you
and all that lies beneath
these surfaces that shield us.

THE PERIODIC TABLE

The twine thin woman,
whose ringless fingers offer
no history lessons, paces before us
in a room where charted science
is taught, where the physical truth,
not the truths we'd rather barter,
is the preferred currency of thought.
Her hands in constant orbit, she weaves
a patient thread through Auschwitz
detainees, Tess Gallagher's cancer,
Chinese women who sold their wartime
hair for rope.

Simple then, to braid hair,
a thousand strands now two plaits
laced across each other like hands
folded in prayer. Simple then,
to gather the lifeline thrown to you,
though the notion of securing this rope
of Mandarin hair makes you shift
in your seat, the tortoise shell
comb in your back pocket now
a terrible conceit.

In America, our president affirms
the cure for terror is shopping.
But for those women whose shaven heads
glistened like freshly cut melons,
their stubby follicles the promise
of seeds among the sweet flesh pulp,
the simple life was a luxury,
its own element, lighter than helium,
colder than carbon, as distant as a mother
lode of gold.

Perched still on laboratory stools,
we raddle the distance between
these women and the one whose hands
cannot light and do not join,
whose voice is now acquainted.
We are ourselves inert, seeking
spaces in the periodic table
so primal they might allow us
the chance to discover
one element that connects us,
a reason to bond.

THIS DOCK, MY HOME

The mistake was thinking
we might measure the journey
in knots, reliant on the wind
and tide to reach hull speed.

We were urged to take to sea
in a glass bottom boat, a monocle
to view the life below us,
curious species not our own.

It never dawned on us
that the abrasion of salt
upon skin, or the slap of wave
against keel wouldn't be

what would knock our sea legs
from us. It is the malaise
that makes us sick, anxious now
to tether our craft, to brace ourselves

against the sycophantic breeze,
to seek the shelter of a slip,
the purl of one man's whistling
the sweetest calling card.

The mistake Otis tells us
is believing the earth spins
in just one direction. To the west,
the sun is sliding into a keyhole

and we remind this King of Soul
this is where he has remained
perched for the past forty years.
I'm here most days, he admits,

though I'm not the one who has
remained the same. You think
it's this mass of land and not
your sloop that are the port of call,

or that's it's on some sidewalk
where you'll catch a falling star.
Rhythm and blues, he croons, rhythm
and blues. Rime from the deep blue sea.

What about *Try a Little Tenderness,*
we submit. Were we supposed to dance
fast or slow? Otis, legs moiling
over the dock like keys

on a player piano, tugs on his beer,
frees the neap foam from his lip, points
to someplace between the sea and
sky. The coast is clear is all

he notes. And it's clear on the coast.
So we won't drop anchor in this bay,
but rather, wait for nightfall,
wait for the stars to align

in constellations we ourselves name.
Look, there's Otis the Soul Man.
And Janis the Siren. And
Icarus the Prodigal Son.

Michael Darcher grew up on the mean cul-de-sacs of Ho-Ho-Kus, New Jersey. Upon turning 18, he fled the confines of metropolitan suburbia for Oregon where he received a BA in English from the University of Portland. Prior to receiving an MFA in Creative Writing and an MA in Literature from the University of Montana, he spent, if that's the right word, a decade as a casino dealer and gaming instructor in Reno, Nevada. Until he retired in 2016, Michael was an English professor at Pierce College, a community college in Washington state, where he taught creative writing and founded *SLAM*, an annual student literary arts magazine that routinely ran in excess of 200 pages and 3,000 copies. His poems and stories have appeared in numerous literary journals including *High Plains Literary Review, Green Mountains Review, The Carolina Quarterly, Crosscurrents, The Nebraska Review, Rio Grande Review*, and elsewhere. One story was nominated for a Pushcart Prize. Michael is presently devoting his attention to seeking representation for two novel manuscripts and crafting new poems. He has never found a suitable answer when asked what he writes about. The best he can do is note that his stories explore what people are willing to do in order to matter, and that he attempts with his poems to place readers in the moment. Many of his poems are the result of eavesdropping without permission into the conversations of others. Michael resides above Commencement Bay in Tacoma with his wife, Joanne, a retired journalism professor, and his 50 lb. love sponge rescue dog, Zelda. Too old and slow to play basketball, he plays as much golf as time and Pacific Northwest weather will allow. For the record, Joanne says she wants to come back in her next life not as Michael's wife but as his dog.